C000110161

TEAM BUILDING

The Principles of Managing People and Productivity

Peter Oliver

TEAM BUILDING

TABLE OF CONTENTS

INTRODUCTION

"Coming together is a beginning. Keeping together is progress. Working together is success." *--Henry Ford*

The Team Building Concise Reads is designed to help you build an effective team. You will learn proven techniques to manage your team and to deliver feedback the right way. You will also learn how valuable performance coaching is, and will get insight into how to identify issues that could impact team dynamics. Are you ready? Let's get started.

People born between 1979 and 1999 account for 50% of the US workforce. What does that mean? It means that the majority of your work team members (and likely including yourself) are millennials. This age group has received a lot of negative press lately but reiterating that won't help us here. The point I'd like you to take away from that magnificent statistic is that the team dynamic and the personal and career fulfillment of each employee is much more important for today's productivity than it was for the baby boomer generation.

An effective manager needs to navigate these new rules of team dynamics if they hope to achieve what they are paid for--results. I love the carrot and stick analogy. If you're not familiar with it, simply said--you can convince a donkey to move forward by either dangling food (carrot) a few feet in front of it or by hitting it on its back with a stick. If you ask most American employees, you will hear them all preferentially ask for the carrot. US corporations responded with sign-on bonuses and end of year bonuses, but it turns out that for today's generation--a bonus at the end of the year is not motivating enough to work through an unfulfilling job. Corporations then came up with the semi-brilliant idea of annual much more frequent 'reviews' or 'feedback sessions'. All that did was reinforce how unfulfilled an employee was with their job. In fact, it wasn't until more recently--literally the past few years that managers began being taught to <u>only</u> give feedback related to someone's <u>strengths</u>.

The reasoning why is ironic. It's not because one is trying to spare the feelings of an employee. There is nothing altruistic in this change in management. Instead, it is because corporations realized the <u>marginal gain</u> they achieve by focusing on <u>strengths</u> rather than <u>weaknesses</u> is several fold higher.

Consequently, companies focus on strengths to maximize productivity gains.

Still...the bonuses, the feedback sessions, these are all 'quick fixes' in terms of improving productivity. As with all concise reads, we want to focus on the principles that have been proven to work. In this book, we will teach you how to manage a team and achieve results as a manager or leader while still making sure everyone feels fulfilled in their careers. It turns out, you need people to achieve results, and you need results to get your job done, so team management is as simple as taking care of the people. Marcus Lemonis, an investor and TV personality emphasizes the three key ingredients for success which are: **People**, Process, and Product. Team building is just a people strategy. Easier said than done, which is why we have to build basic principles and frameworks so that this can be taught to anyone who wants to learn.

BUILDING AN EFFECTIVE TEAM

You've heard me say in other Concise Reads guides that no one is born one way or another and I argue for nurture vs. nature or the belief that habits, thoughts, even personalities can be taught and untaught instead of believing that we are born with a specific predilection and that cannot be changed. I say this because this is exactly what happens in BUILDING an effective team. Notice that I didn't say PICKING an effective team. The resume only tells you if they're qualified for a job. There's still work to be done to build an effective team.

Team Building Framework:

If we pick people we've worked well in the past, we still have to build the team. So how do we BUILD a team regardless of who the team members are? It's easy and I've done it many times in the past. What we need to remember is a simple framework known as the E^3 or E-cubed team framework which consists of Endorsement, Execution, and Excitement.

Endorsement: The team should be aligned in its purpose and its beliefs. Before starting the project, the manager must understand if every team member can easily endorse the project. If they cannot do so readily, then the manager must push to discover the root causes. If the team members (doesn't have to be all, even if it's just one member) cannot readily endorse the project, then the manager should draft a document of guiding principles that members could agree upon. These guiding principles are a <u>proxy for endorsement</u> of the project itself.

For example, let's say that a large corporation is planning a transformation where they have agreed to cut 5% of total running costs by the next 6 months. Some team members might think it is impossible to accomplish, or that cutting costs is against their morale nature if it means that someone down the line such a customer or employee will be affected. Whatever the case may be, they just do not feel comfortable to endorse a cost cutting measure. That's ok to voice by the way, because we want <u>genuine endorsement</u> in order to achieve success. In this situation, we would draft a set of guiding principles that the team can agree on. This set of guiding principles will likely include the following:

- We will strive to make certain the company is in good financial health
- We will make an effort to eliminate up to 5% of waste
- We will work together to find synergistic relationships so that our colleagues do not do the same work or have to do it twice because of poor communication

As you can see, these guiding principles allow for better buy-in, alignment, or endorsement rather than an unfavorable cost-cutting mission.

You must achieve endorsement.

I've seen the consequences of not achieving endorsement early on many times before. Members are assigned to a team but only devote 50% of their energy to execution because they do not truly endorse the mission of the team project.

Execution: This is the second component of building an effective team and it consists of the important tools of feedback and coaching. We touched lightly on feedback and will talk more about it in the next section. In addition to feedback and coaching, an effective team requires clear roles and processes. Processes should be constructed for:

1. Communication

2. Conflict resolution, and

3. Project management tracking.

These three processes should be agreed upon in the endorsement phase and then require periodic check-ins to adjust. In our 'Problem

Solving' Concise Reads guide we learn to deconstruct a problem into its components and assign owners to each component. The process of tracking requires assigned owners and tracking of outputs. Make sure the tracking tool is publically viewable so that every member is not only accountable to you but to the team as well since this is a team effort.

As a manager and leader you will soon realize that you don't need to check in as often as you think you need to once processes are in place for communication, conflict resolution, and project management tracking.

In the 1990s I would have recommended different spreadsheets and tables that have helped me organize and identify these processes for effective execution. However, today it makes no sense to teach you antiquated tools. Instead, I'll let you explore common PM tools such as asana, wrike, trello, basecamp, or jira.

Many of these digital tools are built on the KANBAN method (https://en.wikipedia.org/wiki/Kanban) Which utilizes a Kanban board. Kanban was a visualization originally developed as part of Toyota's lean manufacturing--lean in the sense that it is meant to eliminate waste from multitasking and interruptions. The Kanban board shows the work in progress for each team member, and allows members to pull a workstream that is waiting or pending instead of the manager pushing initiatives onto the team member. Once this is done the member takes ownership of the task and tally of completed initiatives is shown. If a member needs assistance to complete a task, this can also be visualized on the Kanban board.

Excitement: It's been the traditional modus operandi (M.O for short) of business managers to manage TIME. That never worked and only decreased the level of fulfillment an employee received from his or her employment.

In fact, if you look at high churn companies where employees leave after one or more years, you will find that the managers there predominantly manage time.

The manager would check every hour or two by email, instant message, phone call, or in person. Slack has been used more recently for this purpose, but while the tool can be used for good by allowing team members a platform for quick communication, it can also be used for evil when managers ping consistently and the employee begins to build anxiety that they could have missed a message from their manager so they click-check consistently throughout the day.

Some managers will say they have to check in as often as they do because employees are lazy. Well laziness combined with stress will give you an ever poorer quality of work. Sure, the work will be done but it will be of poor quality, and you run the risk of having the employee leave the company and having to retrain another employee.

I've also had other managers tell me, 'Well, I only want employees who want to be here, good riddance to those who left'. That again is a <u>fault of the manager</u> who only manages <u>time</u>.

The employees who stayed really needed the paycheck, otherwise they too would have left.

Purposely having stressed it enough, I believe, that time management is the worst kind of management. I want you to now embrace, endorse, and believe in **ENERGY** management.

As a manager you need to have a pulse check on your team's energy. Are they fulfilled? are they productive? Do they feel conflicted? Is there conflict among them? Do they need external expertise? By feeling the energy of the team, you will be able to adapt and change the team dynamics to constantly boost energy levels in order to maximize productivity. A simple example that occurred just last week was when a member of the team who was responsible for the design of our marketing campaign felt their ideas did not make it to the initial draft and they were less than excited to 'think outside the box' or to be creative. I noticed that when I asked 'Hey Julia, why don't you come up with the colors you think would work in this case. I trust your expertise'. And Julia responded with 'Oh it's ok. If the team lets me know what colors they want, I'll just include those in the design'. That's all it took for me to realize we needed to pause and refresh. So I asked the design team to go through a 48 hour sprint and begin the ideation process from scratch and see if they still align on the current design we've set forth.

The final marketing campaign was a tremendous success, and the biggest feedback from consumers was how much they liked the design!

Managing excitement is extremely important for building an effective team, especially if the project is going to take several weeks or months. Always have a finger on the energy pulse and your team will thank you for it and your boss will thank you even more.

Managing energy instead of time was highlighted in a Harvard Business Review article on a management initiative at Wachovia that saw up to 20% increase in productivity by making sure energy was optimized through education. This is an excerpt on the study design

< https://hbr.org/2007/10/manage-your-energy-not-your-time >

"In early 2006 we took 106 employees at 12 regional banks in southern New Jersey through a curriculum of four modules, each of which focused on specific strategies for strengthening one of the four main dimensions of energy. We delivered it at one-month intervals to groups of approximately 20 to 25, ranging from senior leaders to lower-level managers. We also assigned each attendee a fellow employee as a source of support between sessions. Using Wachovia's own key performance metrics, we evaluated how the participant group performed compared with a group of employees at similar levels at a nearby set of Wachovia banks who did not go through the training. To create a credible basis for comparison, we looked at year-over-year percentage changes in performance across several metrics."

Many Fortune 100 companies have educational modules made available for their employees. Even the American Medical Association requires hospitals to teach their doctors what good sleep hygiene looks like.

This is should be a standard service everywhere (hint for your next startup). This Concise Reads wants you as a future manager and leader to take the fight to the frontline in the workplace.

Team Building Productivity Cycle:

Now that we've learned the three Es of building an effective team, let's now take a look at a the productivity cycle which is standard in today's most productive companies (hence the naming).

Productivity Cycle: This is based on accountability and setting a cadence for the organization. Accountability is important for employees to take ownership of the output and deadlines. Cadence is important as it has been shown that when teams follow a daily or weekly routine, they start to order the way they work so there are fewer delays, interruptions, and idle time. This is more true for teams that require more collaboration than individual work.

The productivity cycle typically consists of regular meetings, manager support, and performance metrics :

1. **Daily stand up meetings or huddles, weekly barometers, and weekly or monthly all-hands sessions:** Whether daily and/or weekly, there is a coming together of all members of a team for an update on what progress each member has made. This can be physical or virtual, but there has to be a sense that an 'update' is due. This sets the internal clock of a team. **Huddles and stand-up meetings** are by definition very short, think--15 minutes on average. This is just to get a pulse on the team process. The longer daily, weekly, or monthly sessions are a great time to identify process problems that are common among team members and to

identify what needs a follow up individual problem solving session. I had several members of a team that found they had a delay in getting financial reports from the finance department in order to set up their marketing and strategy pitch decks. Once that was identified as a process problem, I was able to de-bottleneck it by assigning all requests to go through one liaison in the finance department. The **barometers** should have their own cadence as well, whether daily or weekly, and these are not updates on the team's performance but rather on a team's energy. Are they happy, sad, tired, annoyed? Start with three simple questions for the first barometer and get feedback from the team if other things should be considered when assessing the health of the team.

The first questions can simply be related to three Es:

- Endorsement: Do you feel you and/or your team members are aligned on the same goal and same deadlines?

- Execution: Are the processes in place effective to achieve outcomes? What doesn't work?

- Excitement: Do you feel you have the support of leadership? Do you currently feel the processes in place allow for work/life balance?

2. **Individual problem solving:** Each team member will eventually hit a roadblock. Once identified in the daily or weekly meeting, it needs to be solved <u>together</u> with the team manager. Roadblocks are not something you tell a team member to

go figure out for themselves, because evidence has shown that is when the biggest drop in productivity occurs. Let's also be clear, that 'creative' roadblocks are handled the same way in the sense that the manager helps guide the creative designer in the right direction but doesn't necessarily solve the problem in detail. Once the roadblock appears to be circumvented, and there is a new path forward, then make sure to follow up <u>prior to the next meeting</u> to see if the team member was successful on this new path. Don't give yourself the chance to be disappointed. It will be your fault as manager if you are surprised that the work was not completed. The role of the manager in general and in this individual problem solving is as SUPPORT. Please think of this role in that way if you want to keep your team members on track without destroying their creativity or encroaching on their autonomy. Here are some tips of the trade when problem solving:

- 1) Identify the problem in a SMART way (specific, measurable, actionable, relevant, and timely)
- 2) Don't solve the problem. Support the team member to maintain product/task ownership
- 3) Encourage failure. It's ok not to actually solve the problem during the problem solving session. Encourage the team member to try something and if they find another roadblock to bring it up for another follow up problem solving session.

- 4) If truly at a stand-still, use root cause analysis. If neither you nor the product owner know what to do next, then write out the 4 Ws and H (what, when, where, why, and how), or draw a fishbone diagram starting with the problem and breaking it up into all its components. Simple tools to identify the root cause.

*To learn the principles of problem solving, see the Concise Reads Problem Solving guide.

3. Performance metrics and visual boards: If projects are long, and by long I mean weeks or months, then as a team manager you'll need to set up metrics that are measured with each team update and have a visual board created. These days this can be part of a dashboard or cloud based visual tool.

Performance metrics are specific to the task. For example, if the team goal is to increase customer satisfaction, then one metric could be satisfaction based on weekly survey, or # of customer complaints, or # of products returned per week. If the task is specific to a team member, then it could be customer satisfaction per team member. The performance board gives the manager and importantly the team a <u>visual snapshot</u> of how close the team or team members are to their respective and collective goals. You can always think of the performance board as a flight schedule. Things change all the time, you can have delays or cancelled flights, and this needs to be accessible and visually easy to read. As stated earlier, many of the PM tools include a Kanban board. Explore the tool you currently use. If you don't use one, take a minute to explore the many different tools available such as asana, wrike, trello, basecamp, or jira.

THE FEEDBACK CYCLE

Feedback is a wonderful core part of a
manager's job. Many managers cringe at
having to give feedback. Some because of
altruistic reasons such as not wanting to hurt
their team member's feelings. Others because
they may not like working with their team
member and dread spending 1-on-1 time.

First, feedback is a two-way street. No one is
perfect, and this is a good opportunity for the
manager to get feedback. Feedback sessions
are not a corporate mechanism to make
individuals deeply reflect on their choices. The
purpose is actually to boost productivity of a
team and has been proven to do so. Targeted
feedback helps build trust, encourages skill
development, and leads to a better functioning

team--hence more productive. In this section, we'll learn three key attributes to successful feedback.

1. Have the right attitude going in

2. Appropriately conduct the feedback session

3. Build an environment that encourages <u>more</u> feedback.

Feedback is practiced similar to taking a weekly barometer because they both actually boost productivity in the long run since happy workers are productive workers (Theory Y of management).

Approach to Feedback: First, as a reminder from the previous section, the role of a manager is to <u>support</u>. How you approach feedback, similar to how you set up your team kickoff defines whether the feedback sessions will yield anything or will be an utter waste of time for both parties. You should:

Recognize the other party for their strengths thus far. This is not a compliment sandwich. You should only talk about their **strengths**. It's been shown that the marginal increase in productivity from developing one's strengths is several orders of magnitude higher than from developing one's weaknesses. So for the sake of productivity, focus on how strengths can be improved.

Be prepared to talk about ways their strength can be developed further. Constructive criticism based on a strength will be well received.

Ask them what they need to develop their strengths further, and how you can support them. It is in your best interest to support your team members, but they don't expect that unless you <u>explicitly</u> ask how it is that you or anyone else on the team can support them.

Ask what they would like to improve on. If it is a weakness, then state helpful recommendations that have helped you in the past or connect them with someone who can help. It's ok to advise on weaknesses from a social standpoint as it builds trust, but it is not something you care about <u>going in</u> because it won't affect productivity as much.

Conducting the feedback session: first it is an extroverted trait that many introverts forget, and that is to begin with social niceties. Feedback sessions are extremely stressful especially if you haven't built a trust relationship yet. That is why it is important to ask them about themselves, and learn a little about them. Talk about the weather or the latest news, and then ask "Shall we start with the feedback?". This simple intro to the feedback sessions will put the team member at ease and they will less likely be defensive when you talk about the observations you have of their strengths and how they can improve.

Side note: Some companies believe in being <u>brutally</u> honest. They say things like transparency and truth will lead to improved performance. That's true, but for the untrained manager, it gives them enough of a leash to be their true selfish, impatient, and rude selves. Giving feedback is a trained characteristic. So listen to me, start with the niceties. You are dealing with people, not emotionless robots. Then after you've established trust, you can get to the truth or said less radically, to the root cause of a problem.

During the feedback session:

a. **Listen!** Taking a page out of Buddhism and professional therapy, it turns out that one of the easiest ways to relieve someone's internal suffering, frustrations, and negative emotions is just simply to listen. Listening is so powerful, that you'll see the team member visibly more relaxed after you've let them speak. Listening implies active listening, so if you play with your phone or takes notes during the conversation, then all you're doing is increase the stress level and decrease the chances the team member will be receptive to feedback.

b.   **Provide only 1-2 honest observations**:
No one can listen to more than 1-2 criticisms
in one sitting. The magic number that triggers
an emotional response is usually 3 areas to
improve on. Stay with 1-2 observations, and
make sure they are honest. We all get
triggered by the slightest comment, and I've
heard managers say "I feel like you don't seem
interested or as enthusiastic as other team
members". That is a terrible thing to say,
because it is a reflection of the manager more
than it is of the team member. It also isn't an
actionable observation. How are they going to
'seem' more excited. Instead if they truly are
not excited, then a better question is "I want
to make sure everyone is excited with the
work they're doing. How do you feel, and is
there anything I can do to get your full
support?". If the latter question is asked, then
you will reveal if the employee is actually

excited or not and what action to take to fix it. They may be excited, but the way they look or talk triggered the manager in a negative way. Keep emotions out of the feedback session, and focus on honest observations.

c.   **Maintain a supportive tone**: As you are discussing ways their productivity can be improved or their strengths developed, they could say something that you've already coached them on. In that instance, you could be triggered to move from a supportive tone to an emotional one and blurt out "We already discussed this!". That statement <u>might as well end the conversation</u>. By hearing that you are emotional, the team member will not want to engage with you and their productivity will not improve. Remember, your job is to make sure everyone is doing their best work <u>to the best of their abilities</u>.

The ideal feedback session will therefore be structured in the following format:

i.   Ask to start the feedback session.

ii. Lead with an honest observation (1-2 maximum).

iii. Explain the impact of that observation on the team, client, or productivity.

iv. Explain what it is that you want to achieve. Better team communication, higher productivity.

v.   Ask what their feedback is for you or the project.

vi. Suggest a few solutions and engage in constructive dialogue.

Creating a culture of feedback: to truly make feedback second nature to your management style and part of the organizational values, you'll need to think of feedback as a support tool to team members and to internalize this radical idea that feedback is not about correcting the person but about improving the team's performance.

In that sense you are finding faults in the process and correcting them so everyone can do their best work to the best of their abilities. This also means that feedback is not intended for the poor performers but for everyone.

Everyone gets feedback.

That way, when someone is called in for feedback, they do not approach it in a negative way which will defeat the purpose of feedback. Lastly, and most importantly, to create a culture of feedback is to ALWAYS ASSUME THE BEST OF INTENTIONS.

This is good advice for any communication, always assume the best of intentions. That way, nothing you say will come off as negative or trite.

We live in a society where everyone is innocent until proven guilty, and since 'intent' is very hard to prove, you better believe every team member is innocent and your job is to support them in any way to improve their behavior, productivity, or communication.

Real anecdote: I once had a young MBA graduate join our team. Bright young person, but only 26 years old. We took everyone out for a fun team event, and they made the mistake of drinking too much. What they did next was nothing short of shocking in the corporate world but typical for a young person jut recently joining the workforce.

They slurred and swayed and had their finger pointing at people the whole night. The next day, I had a feedback session with them, pointing out their strengths in building relationships with the team. I pointed out my observation of the previous night, and how that likely impacted their present and future relationships with the team. I then told them what I wanted, which was for stronger team relationships for better collaboration. I paused (for effect). I then asked for the young person's feedback. They explained that it was not their intention to ruin relationships, that they hope this does not get them fired because they really like the job and want to do the best they can. I then engaged with the young person to find ways to prevent this behavior from happening in the future and ways to improve the relationships in the team right now. We agreed on the next steps, and I asked if it was ok to meet again in a week and see how what progress has been made. They left feeling supported, and after apologizing to the team, we soon discovered a productive and helpful team member. I used my position as a supportive platform and assumed they had the best intentions. After all, our frontal cortex only barely finished developing by 26 anyways, but still--professionally this could have cost them their job somewhere else and a team would have lost one its most collaborative members. Note, that their age was not factored in. Statistically, it's just more likely a younger person would be receiving this feedback session.

PERFORMANCE COACHING

While feedback is a static point in time, coaching is continuous. The goal of effective coaching is to improve performance. Similar to athletic coaching, there is an element of motivational coaching, but management coaches go a step beyond that. They use specific observations, active listening, and thoughtful questioning to lead their team members to identify constructive ways they can improve their performance. In this section, we'll learn a framework for coaching sessions as well as learn to appreciate how the popular Socrates method of questioning helps promote self-discovery in the team member.

How it differs from feedback: We've previously learned that in feedback sessions, the manager first asks permission, then shares an observation and the impact to the team, pauses to gather feedback from the team member, and then begins brainstorming for possible solutions. Coaching is an extended feedback session in that it occurs over a longer period of time with the goal of improving overall performance and team alignment and execution.

Let's look at an example with the basic coaching framework.

Share An Observation: A manager observes that a team member is slow to accomplish goals during the day when surrounded with other team members but in the middle of the night sends emails with completed work. The manager shares this observation with the team member.

Manager: John, I've noticed that you are less productive during the day but at night when you are alone you accomplish the goals of the day.

Use The Socrates Method Of Questioning: The manager then asks the team member a series of questions in response to the team member's answers. For example:

Manager: John, do you prefer working at night instead of during the day?

John: Yes I would, but I'm actually more tired at night, and I'm afraid I may make a mistake.

Manager: Why are you tired at night?

John: Because I spend the better part of the day helping others with their work

Manager: Do you find that because you help others with their work, you have little time to finish your own work?

John: Yes, but I know I can always get to it after hours and I don't want to seem like I'm not a team player.

Manager: I think helping others is a great quality to have, but how can we change the work environment so it does not prevent you from finishing your work? I think your expertise is helpful to the team, but I also do not want you to work overtime, so let's find something that works for everyone.

John: I find that when I'm interrupted throughout the day, it takes me longer to accomplish my tasks. Maybe if I was interrupted less often?

Manager: Are the interruptions for similar reasons or are they different?

John: Most are for the same reason.

Brainstorm An Action Experiment: The manager then makes sure to conclude the coaching session with a plan of action. Similar to a singular feedback session, the **intent** is to support the team member and to approach the coaching sessions assuming the team member has the best of intentions. It is critical to have the right mindset when coaching.

Manager: Do you think you would be able to finish your tasks during the day if we scheduled interruptions to a specific time of day?

John: Yes, and also if we had a communication tool so other team members could see my answers to a previously asked question then that would significantly reduce the interruptions.

Manager: Ok, that sounds like a plan. What did you have in mind?

John: Maybe we could use Slack or another messaging platform, and I could answer questions only between 8-10 am each morning?

Manager: That sounds like an experiment we can try. Let's revisit how that works after putting it in place for a week.

The above scenario is adapted from the original **GROW** framework used in fortune 500 organizations. GROW stands for **Goal** (neutral observation), **Reality** (active listening and questioning), **Options** (brainstorming solutions), and **Way forward** (decide on an action plan and follow up conversation).

Socratic Paradox: Socrates, the ancient Greek Philosopher, wanted to test the Oracle of Delphi's assertion that he is the wisest man alive. Thus, he went to all the great experts in Athens and asked them a question which they answered. He then followed up with subsequent questions until finally each expert reached a point where they didn't have an answer. At that point it is said that he truly believed he is the wisest man alive because as he said "I know that I know nothing". What is interesting about Socrates is that he really wasn't an expert in anything. Literally, nothing! He wasn't a Leonardo Da Vinci or a polymath. However, he was wise because he knew that he knew nothing. It is that knowledge that makes it impressive to watch Socrates ask question after question to experts, knowing full well that he does not possess any answers, and for the sole purpose of pushing the expert to really articulate their position and through that gain a better understanding of themselves.

I mention the Socratic Paradox, because it reinforces the role of the coach. As a manager and leader, you may often at times not have any solutions or answers and must approach the coaching session with observations only.

That is how it should be. It is the process of active listening and questioning, all in the spirit of support, that will help the team member discover the root cause of any observation.

Just like Socrates, you can know nothing about anything and still be an effective coach.

Powerful insight, I know. Just don't advertise to your boss that you know noting.

TEAM DYNAMICS

Now that you're an expert in the basics of individual feedback and coaching for team members. It is time to connect this to the broader team dynamics. In this concise section, we'll look at identifying the common ways teams underperform and appreciating that like feedback and coaching, this requires an action plan to get the team aligned in its goals, and capable of executing on these goals.

The first step in effective team dynamics is **gathering anonymous feedback** in the form of a survey.

If you google 'team dynamics survey' you'll see hundreds of different surveys, some only 5 questions long, others 50 questions long. Each prompt is a question asking to rate a particular team attribute or a statement asking to rate how much a team members agrees or disagrees. Here is a very simple team dynamic survey with a rating from 0 for completely disagree to 5 for completely agree:

1. The team is aligned in their goals and have adequately scoped the problem and the way forward.
2. Each member of the team knows and understand their role.
3. Team members find support from each other to complete their work.
4. Team members are comfortable raising issues or offering their opinions in open communication.
5. Leadership is supportive and is actively involved in helping the team achieve their goals.

6. The team is effective in identifying roadblocks early on.

7. The team executes its tasks in an organized and timely fashion.

8. Team members feel they are having a positive impact and that their work will have a positive impact.

9. The team has processes in place to prevent burnout and promote professional and personal life balance.

A common result from these team dynamic surveys is poor alignment from the start of the team engagement. **Poor alignment** on scope and role leads to siloed work, more frequent roadblocks, and repetitive work. Poor alignment along with **lack of open communication**, and **burnout** from imbalanced priorities leads to poor execution of intended goals. That is why, the bulk of effective team dynamics start with proper alignment which is discovered through the team dynamics survey.

We learned how effective barometers can be for small group productivity. This is even more important with larger teams, and you could think of a team survey as a larger, less frequent, and more comprehensive team barometer that looks at how individuals work together rather than how individuals feel regarding their own work environment.

Although obvious, it should be stated. The results of the team dynamics survey **must** be shared with the team to brainstorm constructive solutions moving forward. The manager **must not** keep these results to themselves with the intention of making unilateral changes.

Conclusion

Team building is an important skill for every manager and leader. There was a lot of information for a one hour read, but let's remember the important points again.

Building a team requires us to start with the three E's framework for Endorsement, Execution, and Excitement. Focusing on energy management and not time management is a 21st century innovation that has been proven to be a win-win for both the company and the employees. Once framework is established we manage a team using the productivity lifecycle which has been show to improve...productivity. This consists of periodic check-ins, problem solving bottlenecks, and productivity metrics. Agile sprints use the Kanban boards to visualize team progress and limit interruptions. We then learn that building a team is not only about putting processes in place but requires active management in the form of feedback sessions. We went through the right way of conducting a feedback session and extended the concept to include coaching which is a never ending continuous process. Remember the manager's job is to support. Lastly, we managing larger teams, team dynamics play a role, and in that case the barometer is expanded to a team survey and the individual feedback session is expanded to an open team discussion.

Hopefully, this has been helpful. Good luck, and pick up your next copy of Concise Reads to acquire new lessons and skills in business.

--The End--

Printed in Great Britain
by Amazon

42764969R00036